## Advanced Picture Concepts

Written by: Bright Kids NYC Inc.
Book Cover by: Carol Hampshire
Illustrations by: Robert Schoolcraft
Published by: Bright Kids NYC Inc.

Bright Kids NYC Inc.
225 Broadway, Suite 3104
New York, New York 10007

Phone: 917-539-4575
Email: info@brightkidsnyc.com
www.brightkidsnyc.com

## TABLE OF CONTENTS

Advanced Picture Concepts

## About Bright Kids NYC

Bright Kids NYC was founded in New York City to provide language arts and math enrichment for young children and to educate parents about standardized tests through workshops and consultations, as well as to prepare young children for such tests through assessments, tutoring and publications. Our philosophy is that regardless of age, test taking is a skill than can be acquired and mastered through practice.

At Bright Kids NYC, we strive to provide the best learning materials. Our publications are truly unique. First, all of our books have been created by psychologists, learning specialists and teachers. Second, our books have been tested by hundreds of children in our tutoring practice. Since children can make associations adults sometimes cannot, testing of materials by children is critical to creating successful test preparation guides. Finally, our learning specialists and teaching staff have provided practical strategies and advice so parents can best help their child prepare to compete successfully on standardized tests.

Feel free to contact us should you have any questions.

Bright Kids NYC Inc.
225 Broadway, Suite 3104
New York, New York 10007

Email: info@brightkidsnyc.com
Phone: 917-539-4575
www.brightkidsnyc.com

Advanced Picture Concepts

## Introduction

This book is designed to help children practice the skills needed to perform well on the Picture Concepts subtest of the ERB/WISC-IV and ERB-WPPSI-III admission tests. Practicing these skills ahead of time will build confidence that will enable children to perform to the best of their ability on test day.

We have used feedback from parents, teachers and students to prepare this book. The content has been generated by our psychologists, learning specialists, and teachers. The activities have been rigorously tested in our tutoring practice and fine-tuned based on practical use with hundreds of young children.

Most importantly, we provide strategies created and used by our staff of trained teachers, which can empower parents to work successfully with their own children. We have included day-to-day activities you can do with your child to further build knowledge and confidence, and many of these strategies will help your child practice the critical thinking skills necessary for future success.

Advanced Picture Concepts

## Why Use a Tutor?

We developed this book to give parents and children the opportunity to work together and practice important skills when tutors are not present. However, we still believe that trained staff of experienced teachers can further enhance each child's learning experience, especially if a busy schedule makes it difficult for parents to find the time for test preparation.

With their extensive knowledge of child development, our tutors dynamically tailor lessons to suit the learning style of each individual child. In addition, our tutors use a variety of supplemental activities and games so that children can learn important concepts in different contexts and formats. Most importantly, all of our tutors are very familiar with the format of the test; they know how the questions will be posed and they can accurately simulate the test-taking experience.

Since someone who is a stranger to your child administers the test, having a tutor presents an excellent opportunity for your child to practice spending an hour with an unfamiliar adult. Some children tend to be less cooperative or not as focused when working with a close family member.

Regardless, children will benefit from practice with the concepts presented in this book whether you choose to use a tutor or to prepare your child without professional support.

# PICTURE CONCEPTS

## Description

Picture concepts are essentially types of classification problems. Initially, children need to choose two items, one from each row, that have a common characteristic. Later questions require them to find three or four items, one from each row.

There are 28 questions on the actual test and the starting point varies based on the child's age. Regardless of the starting point, children first complete two trial items before they start the test. The Picture Concepts subtest is discontinued after five consecutive scores of zero.

## Instructions

SAY: Look at the first row (point to the first row). Then look at the second row (point to the second row).

SAY: Can you find one object from each row and tell me how they are connected to each other?

(If answer is incorrect)

SAY: Let's try again. A duck does not go with a fire hydrant as well as with a goose, because ducks and geese are both birds. Do you see why these are the two items that go together?

Continue with all the exercises in the same manner. Picture Concepts with four rows are designated primarily for older children.

## Strategies

1. Make sure you explain to your child that he or she needs to pick only one item from each row. This is a major area of confusion and many children are uncomfortable with the format.

2. Make sure your child explains his or her choice out loud, even if it is correct.

3. Help your child understand that items can have multiple relationships. If he or she cannot find a match, he or she may have to look for another characteristic that are common to the items.

4. Pay attention to the shape and texture of objects pictured. Common characteristics may include physical traits as well as category, function, and purpose such as items that are made of metal, items that are hot or cold etc.

# PICTURE CONCEPTS

# EXERCISES

Advanced Picture Concepts

**1**

**2**

**3**

**4**

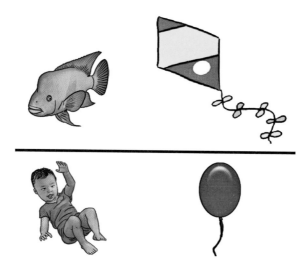

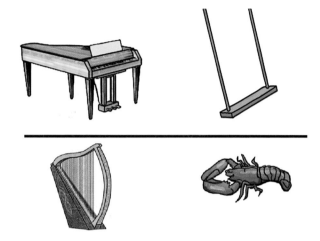

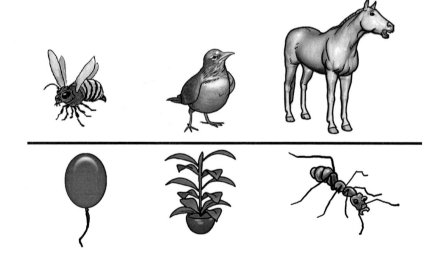

**7**

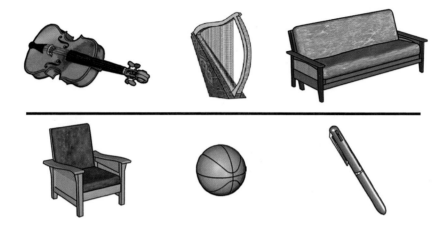

**8**

Advanced Picture Concepts     Bright Kids NYC Inc. ©

**9**

**10**

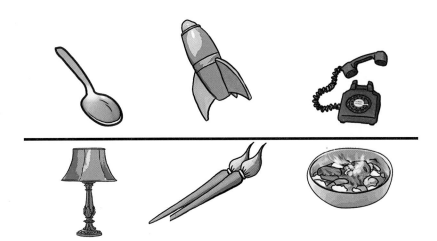

**11**

**12**

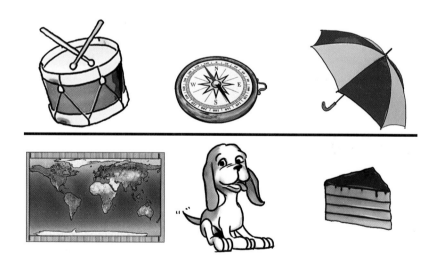

Advanced Picture Concepts

**13**

**14**

**15**

**16**

Advanced Picture Concepts · Bright Kids NYC Inc. ©

**17**

**18**

**19**

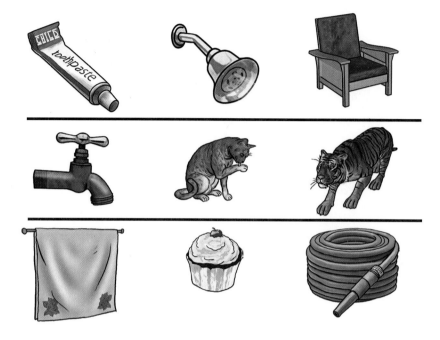

**20**

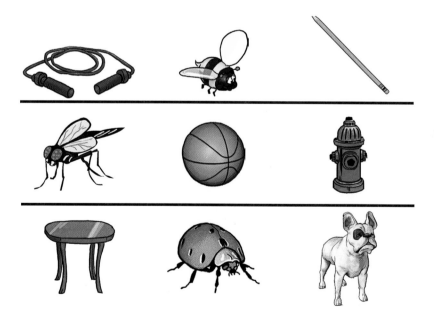

Advanced Picture Concepts

**21**

**22**

**23**

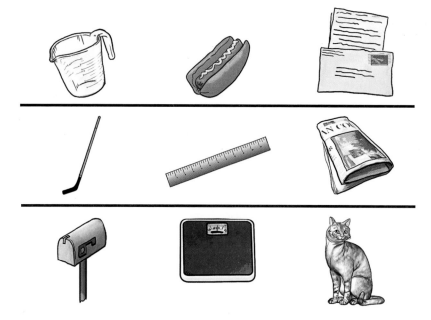

**24**

Advanced Picture Concepts

**25**

**26**

**27**

**28**

Advanced Picture Concepts

**29**

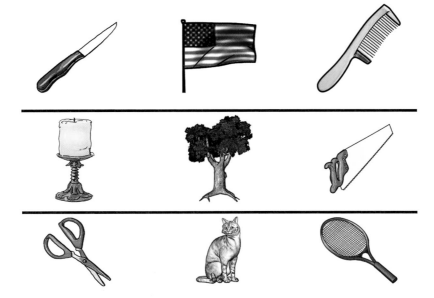

**30**

Advanced Picture Concepts

# PICTURE CONCEPTS

# EXERCISES

# (Advanced)

Advanced Picture Concepts

**31**

**32**

Advanced Picture Concepts

Bright Kids NYC Inc. ©

**33**

**34**

Advanced Picture Concepts    Bright Kids NYC Inc. ©

# PICTURE CONCEPTS - ANSWER KEY

1. DUCK and GOOSE

2. BOOK and NEWSPAPER

3. CANDLE and LAMP

4. KITE and BALLOON

5. PIANO and HARP

6. BEE and ANT

7. SOFA and CHAIR

8. POLICE CAR and POLICEMAN

9. BASEBALL BAT and TENNIS RACQUET

10. SPOON and SOUP

11. GRAPES and APPLE

12. COMPASS and MAP

13. BELL and TELEPHONE

14. DOLL and TOY TRAIN

15. FIRE HYDRANT and FIRE HOSE

16. SHEET OF MUSIC and GUITAR

17. STAMP and ENVELOPE

18. PAPER and TREE

19. SHOWERHEAD and FAUCET and HOSE

# PICTURE CONCEPTS – ANSWER KEY (Cont.)

20. BEE and MOSQUITO and LADYBUG

21. TOP HAT and BASEBALL HAT and CONSTRUCTION HAT

22. BOOK and FAN and DOLLAR BILL

23. MEASURING CUP and RULER and SCALE

24. ROCKET and HELICOPTER and HOT AIR BALLOON

25. EARTH and BASKETBALL and FERRIS WHEEL

26. PENGUIN and IGLOO and SNOWMAN

27. GARBAGE CAN and ROBOT and NAIL

28. TENT and PYRAMID and PARTY HAT

29. KNIFE and SAW and SCISSORS

30. FROG and SNAKE and TURTLE

31. WATER BOTTLE and FISH BOWL and BATHTUB

32. ROWBOAT and RAFT and SHIP

33. TENNIS RACQUET and GOLF CLUB and HOCKEY STICK

34. WINDMILL and HELICOPTER and FERRIS WHEEL